Amazing
Wolves
Dogs & Foxes

WRITTEN BY
MARY LING

PHOTOGRAPHED BY
JERRY YOUNG

DK

599.7444 (5)

DORLING KINDERSLEY
London · New York · Stuttgart

A Dorling Kindersley Book

Project editor Louise Pritchard
Art editor Ann Cannings
Senior editor Helen Parker
Senior art editor Jacquie Gulliver
Production Louise Barratt

Illustrations by Angelika Elsbach, Julie Anderson,
John Hutchinson, Dan Wright
Animals supplied by Trevor Smith's Animal World,
Duisburger Zoo, Germany,
Editorial consultants The staff of the Natural History Museum, London
Special thanks to Carl Gombrich and Kate Raworth for research

First published in Great Britain in 1991 by
Dorling Kindersley Limited
9 Henrietta Street, London WC2E 8PS

A CIP catalogue record for this book is available from the British Library

ISBN 0 86318 626 2

Colour reproduction by Colourscan, Singapore
Printed in Italy by A. Mondadori Editore, Verona

Contents

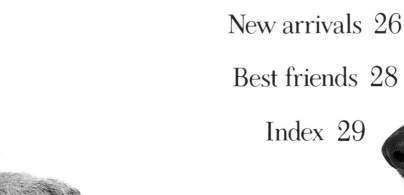

Running wild

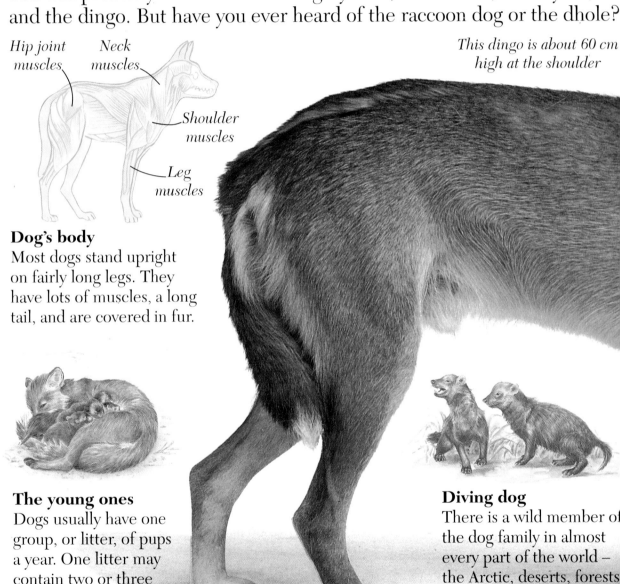

The pet dog has about 35 wild relations in the dog family. You will probably have heard of the grey wolf, the red fox, the coyote, and the dingo. But have you ever heard of the raccoon dog or the dhole?

Hip joint muscles

Neck muscles

Shoulder muscles

Leg muscles

This dingo is about 60 cm high at the shoulder

Dog's body

Most dogs stand upright on fairly long legs. They have lots of muscles, a long tail, and are covered in fur.

The young ones

Dogs usually have one group, or litter, of pups a year. One litter may contain two or three pups or as many as ten or twelve. The pups are looked after until they can hunt for themselves.

Diving dog

There is a wild member of the dog family in almost every part of the world – the Arctic, deserts, forests and towns. Some are good at climbing or swimming. The bush dog of South America dives underwater.

Gone wild
Aborigines brought the dingo to Australia as a hunting companion long ago. Now the dingo is wild.

Pointed teeth for stabbing prey

Strong teeth for chewing

Snap happy
Dogs are carnivores, which means they eat meat. They have strong jaws and teeth for tearing, grinding, and chewing.

Face like a dog
As well as barking, dogs talk with their faces, tails, and bodies. These wolves are arguing, and the one on the right is saying, "You win!"

Packing them in
Many wild dogs live together in packs. There are strict rules within the pack and every member knows its place.

Muddy paws
A dog cannot tuck away its blunt, sturdy nails the way a cat pulls in its claws. These wolf paw marks clearly show the print of nails in the mud.

9

Top dog

Wolves are the largest members of the dog family. There are two kinds of wolf – the grey wolf and the red wolf. Sadly, the red wolf is almost extinct.

What big teeth

The wolf's sharp teeth are ideal for catching and eating large animals such as deer or elk. But it also eats rabbits, snakes, insects, and even fruit.

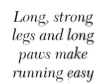

Hungry to kill

Wolves only hunt when they are hungry. Most scary stories about wolves attacking people are not true. Healthy wolves do not attack humans unless they have a good reason.

On the run

Wolves are great runners and can keep up a steady pace for many hours. One red wolf in America didn't stop running for two weeks. It covered about 200 km.

Foot paces

Wolves usually trot from place to place or run in a way called loping. But in a chase they can reach speeds of up to 65 km/h in short bursts.

Long, strong legs and long paws make running easy

Wolf power

Grey wolves can have black, white, or grey fur, depending on where they live. This male grey wolf is about 1 m tall at the shoulder. Female wolves are usually slightly smaller than the males.

Wolves have a very good sense of smell for sniffing out prey

Moonlighting

Stories are told of people that turn into wolves after dark and terrify the neighbours. They are called werewolves. Don't worry – they are only make-believe.

Cry wolf

Many people are scared by the sound of wolves howling. But the wolves are only keeping in touch with each other or telling other packs they are there.

11

Town and country

The cunning red fox has learnt to change its habits to suit its surroundings. Now it is as happy living in towns as in the countryside.

High jumps

Foxes can catch small animals by springing into the air and pouncing on them. The foxes pin their victims to the ground with their front paws.

Fast food

Dustbins are good places for the streetwise fox to find a takeaway meal. But it should learn to clear up afterwards!

Lofty perch

The red fox is not an expert climber but it is good enough to be able to find a safe place to sleep after a night out.

Safe at home

When cubs are due, the mother fox, or vixen, looks for a hole underground to give birth. The fox's home is called an earth and the cubs can keep safe inside.

Fox about town

More and more foxes are seen in towns. They live in large gardens and parks or by railway lines, and make their earths in sheds, cellars, or even drains.

A useful brush

A fox's tail is called a brush, but it is not used for sweeping the floor. The mother fox flicks her tail to warn her cubs of danger, and a tail makes a cosy blanket in chilly weather.

Autumn feast
Foxes are happy
to eat fruit when
meat is in short
supply. Juicy berries
are hard to resist –
and much easier to
catch than run-
away mice.

*This red fox
is about
110 cm long,
from the tip of
its nose to the
tip of its tail*

Lone ranger
Red foxes hunt on their
own, not in a pack. But related females
may help to look after the cubs.

Life on ice

Temperatures in the Arctic can fall so low that humans would be frozen stiff. But animals such as the Arctic fox are specially designed to survive the severe cold.

Deep freeze
Arctic foxes like to keep a store of food buried for times when prey is scarce. One fox was found with forty birds and over thirty eggs in the "freezer".

Snow white fox
Arctic foxes have thick, soft fur to keep them warm. In the winter most of them have a white coat. They are then perfectly hidden in the snowy landscape.

On the scrounge
As well as hunting for themselves, Arctic foxes often tag along behind polar bears and pick up any of the bears' leftovers.

Summer clothes
This Arctic fox is wearing its smoky-grey summer suit. When the snow melts in the spring, the fox does not need to be white any more.

Short rounded ears lose less heat than long ears

This Arctic fox is about 30 cm tall

Alarm call

A vole hibernating under the snow may get a nasty shock if a hungry Arctic fox sniffs it out. The fox reaches the vole by jumping up and down to break the ice.

Winter diet

The Arctic wolf is a type of grey wolf with rounded ears and usually a white coat. It normally hunts moose and caribou, but in winter, when food is scarce, it sometimes has to settle for smaller prey, like this Arctic hare.

Feet are lined with fur to save heat

New arrivals

As spring arrives, many animals settle in one place to raise a family.

Hot dogs

You may think that dogs could not possibly live in hot or dry places like tropical forests or deserts. They do – although some are hardly ever seen.

Trapped in fur
A fox cannot take off its coat when it is too hot. So the kit fox, like many other animals that live in hot places, has big ears which let body heat escape.

This Ruppell's fox is about 45 cm long with a 30-cm-long tail

Secret hunter
Few people have seen the small-eared zorro. It only lives in the Amazon rainforest in South America. It hunts for food on its own – and only at night.

Out of the sun
The fennec fox is the smallest fox in the world. It lives in the Sahara Desert, where it rests under rocks to hide from the heat of the day. In the cooler evenings, the fox comes out to hunt for insects.

Foot pads
Foxes that live in deserts have fur-lined feet. This lets them walk across the baking-hot sand or rock without burning their toes.

Hot snacks
The Australian outback can be very hot and dry. It may seem like an empty larder to us, but dingoes can usually find something to eat. This one has found a monitor lizard in one of the water holes.

Large ears for hearing and keeping cool

Well-hidden
The brownish-grey coat of Blanford's fox hides it among the rocks where it lives. Blanford's fox is one of four kinds of fox called desert foxes. The others are the pale, Ruppell's, and the fennec.

Furry fox
Ruppell's fox lives in stony or sandy deserts. Its sand-coloured coat looks soft and thick – and it is!

17

Howls and growls

Woofs and barks don't mean much to us, but dogs understand them. Each kind of dog has its own language which varies, even from pack to pack.

Monkeying around

When African wild dogs are playing, they often whimper or chatter. They can sound very un-dog-like and much more like monkeys.

Baby talk

A wolf is never too young to howl! Grey wolf pups call to their friends too.

A far cry

A pack of howling wolves can be heard by humans as far as 16 km away. All the members of the pack want to join in and any other packs in an area of 300 sq km will get the message to keep away.

Howdy coyote

A howling coyote stars in most westerns. Its call is a series of yelps and a long wail. It's not trying to scare cowboys. It's only claiming its territory.

Dog with no bark

Dingoes may look like ordinary dogs but unlike them, they hardly ever bark! They howl and yelp and make all sorts of other noises instead.

Whistle stop

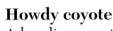

You may have heard of a dog-whistle, but have you heard of a whistling dog? Dholes often whistle to the rest of the pack when they want to re-group after a failed hunt.

Telling the neighbours
The grey fox often climbs trees – an unusual habit for a fox. It is often called the tree fox. It's no secret when a grey fox is ready to mate. Its piercing screams reach every fox in its territory.

This handsome grey fox is about 37 cm tall at the shoulder

When climbing, the front paws grip, the back paws push

The pack goes hunting

 Most wolves and wild dogs live in packs. They travel, rest, and hunt together. The pack is led by the strongest and bravest individuals – and they may be asked to prove it.

Stalking

Once African wild dogs are within 500 m of their prey, they begin to stalk, ears back, and head lowered. When the chase begins the dogs can keep running for 2 or 3 km at about 50 km/h.

Hanging on

With a powerful leap, the leading dog jumps at the nose or throat of the fleeing animal. The dog will hang on, no matter what, until the other dogs come to help.

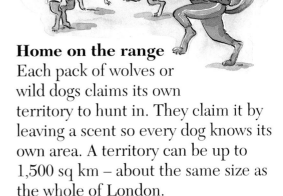

Home on the range

Each pack of wolves or wild dogs claims its own territory to hunt in. They claim it by leaving a scent so every dog knows its own area. A territory can be up to 1,500 sq km – about the same size as the whole of London.

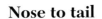

Baby food

After a kill, adults bring food back for the pups. This may be a piece of skin or a bone, or the dogs may regurgitate (bring up) meat they've already chewed, which is easier for young pups to eat.

Nose to tail

When hunting in freezing snow, wolves walk in single file. They take it in turns to lead and make tracks for the others to walk in.

Eating alone
Jackals may go hunting in family groups for large animals. But often they make it clear they would rather be alone at meal-times!

This African wild dog is about 65 cm tall

A family affair
A pack of African wild dogs can contain more than sixty animals, but the average number is ten. All the males, and usually all the females, are related.

Amazing senses

Dogs survive by using their senses, especially sight, hearing, and smell. With their senses they can tell friend from foe, find food, and leave and pick up messages.

Scratch and sniff

Wolves mark trees on their trails with urine, just as pet dogs do. A male wolf will often scrape a mark on the ground too, so that other wolves will see that it's his trail even if they don't smell it.

Ears to the ground

Dogs have much better hearing than humans. If you were a wolf or a fox, you would be able to hear a watch ticking 10 m away. This bat-eared fox can even hear insects moving.

Past master

A dog does not need to have photographs to build up a picture of the past. It uses its strong sense of smell to find out who has been there before it.

Touching scene

Mouths and teeth are fierce tools for catching food, but they are also used gently for carrying pups or for grooming. This jackal family shows affection by grooming each other.

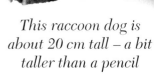

This raccoon dog is about 20 cm tall – a bit taller than a pencil

What big ears you have!
In the fairy tale of Little Red Riding Hood, the big bad wolf pretends to be the little girl's grandmother. But he finds it hard to disguise his large ears and eyes.

This raccoon dog looks as if it has a black mask on its face – just like a raccoon

Wide-eyed
The fennec fox has large eyes and can see in the dark. This is useful to the fox when it's out at night, hunting insects and other small animals for its dinner.

Sensible dog
The raccoon dog obviously feels the cold. It is the only dog that sleeps through much of the winter. This is called hibernating.

Dogs in danger

Living in the wild is not always easy. For some dogs it has become a struggle to survive. Some catch diseases, some have their homes destroyed by people, and many are hunted for their fur.

Stop, thief!
Simien jackals live in Ethiopia in Africa. They are nearly extinct as farmers are taking over the land where they live and hunt for food.

Driven out
People are taking over the savanna home of the African wild dog, leaving deserts and swamps for it to hunt in. With too little food, many wild dogs have died.

Wolf watch
The red wolf is so rare it is almost extinct. People are trying to help the red wolf increase its numbers by breeding it in zoos. When the puppies can look after themselves they are put into the wild.

Tree den
The short-legged bush dog is very rare. It lives in groups of up to ten and makes its den in burrows or hollow trees.

Forest dogs
Asian red dholes live in rainforests. But these forests are being cut down to make farmland, leaving fewer places where the dholes can live.

Whose coat is it?
Many foxes, wolves, jackals, and other dogs are dying out because they are hunted by people. Some are killed by farmers who think they are a nuisance, and many are killed just to make fur coats.

Oil or nothing
San Joaquin kit foxes live among oil fields in California, USA, and are surrounded by cotton farms. Now there are only about 7,000 of these kit foxes left.

In name only
The rare maned wolf of central South America is not a wolf. It was given this name because of its large size. It is often described as a fox on stilts! If it is scared by an enemy, it raises its long mane to make it look bigger.

On its long legs, this maned wolf is about 80 cm high at the shoulder

New arrivals

Young wolves, dogs, and foxes may not have to go to school, but they still have a lot of learning and growing to do before they can look after themselves.

Born blind
Puppies are born blind. A newborn red fox is about the size of a mole. It has short fluffy fur and cuddles up to its mother to keep warm.

Too young
This grey wolf cub is about eight weeks old. He will not join the rest of the pack on a hunting trip until he is six months old.

This young wolf cub is about 35 cm tall

Wolf protector

In legend, Romulus and Remus were twin brothers brought up by a wolf. She must have taught them well – Romulus founded the city of Rome in Italy in 753 B.C.

Mother's milk

At first, puppies drink only their mother's milk, just as human babies do. Mother's milk is full of goodness to build up the puppies' strength.

Meat eaters

When they are only a few weeks old, African wild dogs get a taste for meat. They love to eat pieces regurgitated by their parents.

Rough and tumble

Rolling and tumbling together is good fun but it is also practice for life as an adult. If there aren't any brothers or sisters to play with, Mum will usually do!

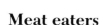

A long way to go

Puppies are smaller all over than adults. They have smaller ears, shorter noses, and shorter legs, The legs of a maned wolf pup have to grow lots before the pup looks like its parents!

A helping paw

Young jackals often stay to help look after newborn brothers and sisters before leaving home. More puppies survive if the mother has help. The helper can also pick up hints which may come in useful when it raises its own family.

Best friends

Pet dogs are all descended from wolves. Humans and wolves became hunting companions as long ago as the Stone Age. Dogs have been helping humans to hunt and herd for thousands of years.

Sheep leaper

The kelpie of Australia is partly descended from the wild dingo. It has an unusual way of moving among the sheep. It leaps on the back of the sheep and runs around on top of their broad fleece!

Smelly job

The German shepherd has been bred to look like its wolf ancestors. It has a good sense of smell and is often used by the police to sniff out explosives and drugs.

Call of the wild

Some dogs have returned to living in the wild. Pariah dogs of Asia usually scavenge around villages but they are not owned by anyone and they live and breed like wild animals.

Dog power

The husky is a wolf-like dog with a thick woolly coat. It pulls sleds across the snow and helps with hunting and herding. In North America it also pulls sleds in races. This husky is about 60 cm tall.

Dog god

The Ancient Egyptians used dogs for hunting. They also had a god called Anubis who they believed was half dog and half jackal.

Ancient breed

Many breeds of dog developed in ancient times. For example, the mastiff was bred from fierce dogs as a guard dog, and the greyhound was bred from fast dogs for hunting.

Out hunting

A bull terrier may not look like a wolf but it has a hunting instinct, handed down to it from its wolf ancestors. It would be happy to join some friends for a hunting trip – if it was allowed to!

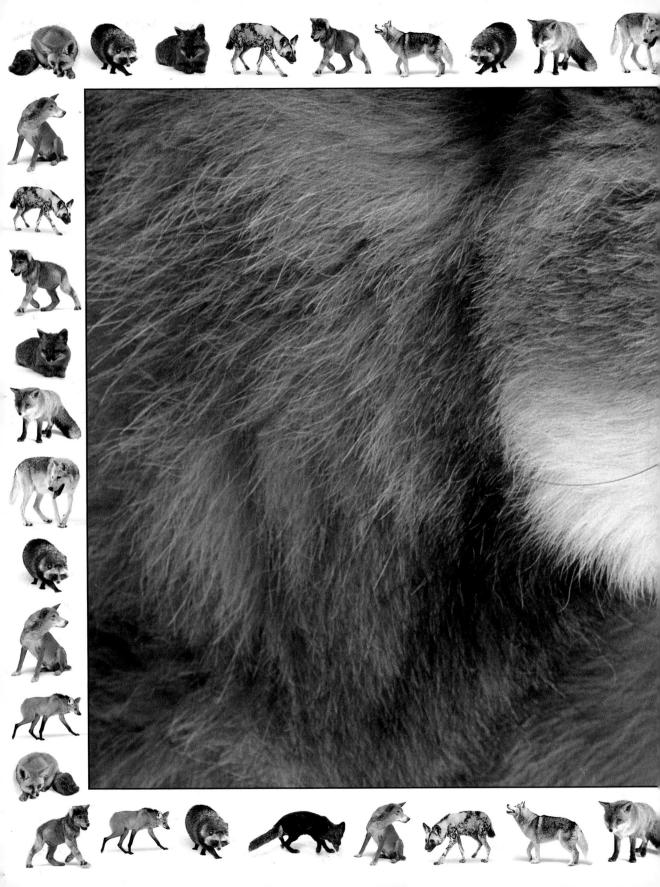